F.L.U.

"Inspirational storyteller; highly recommended"

Unless otherwise indicated, all Scripture quotations are taken from the King James and The Living Word versions of the Bible.

F.L.U.

ISBN: 978-0-9914975-0-8

Copyright © 2013 by Karen Alexander

Published by Karen Alexander
Mobile, AL
Editor: Michiel E. Cook
Cover Design: India M. Burns

Printed in the United States of America.

DEDICATION

This book is dedicated to my family for encouraging me to do what I love; especially Cameron for always saying "keep writing mom," and my mother and father for showing me how to love with no boundaries.

Baby Girl 🖤

TABLE OF CONTENTS

Forward

Failure of Living Up ("F.L.U.") is an encouraging, motivational and inspiring message that helps us live up to our greatest potential in life. It is an easy read with plenty of inspirational stories that can be applied to any given situation in someone's life and make a person really think about how to take that potential and become successful. Since the last word of this book I have thought endlessly about what my gifts and talents are. I am happy say I have discovered a few I knew of but put aside, but also found some new talents and gifts. Glad I read it from cover to cover. HIGHLY RECOMMENDED.

- MICHIEL E. COOK
        Editor

Preface

It's January 23rd. My birthday is over and I am now a wondering forty-two. This is the beginning of my wondering story.

I saw a young handsome man standing in a music store in the mall. Even though the stare only lasted for a moment, not even long enough for our eyes to meet, it seemed as if it lasted for hours. As I walked past the store with my eyes set on McDonald's as my destination for lunch, a strong, what almost could be described as angelic, thought quickly went through my mind saying, "That's going to be your husband." I thought that this wistful thinking was absolutely crazy and my mind must be in a playful mood today. After all, he did not have the usual physical features needed for a man to catch my interest. The most obvious feature that was not typical for me was that he was short, yet he was very handsome. Even though I frequent this store to buy the $1.00 cassette tapes at least twice a week (you know you could do that back in the day), I had never met him before. As I was returning from lunch, I stopped in to see what new tapes were in. He walked up to me and offered his assistance and I immediately declined. Now, I am not sure if he asked me if I worked in the mall or if I was wearing a name tag that indicated where I worked, but this was the beginning of a long story.

A couple of days later, as I was working in the linen department of a local retail store, I was approached by a familiar face and asked for my assistance. He had such a smooth, tauntingly chocolate skin tone. Oh, I wanted him so bad that my body felt numb. Even though neither of us openly acknowledged our attraction to each other, the chemistry was real, and it was flowing. He purchased his inviting bedding set and left with a seductive smile and a "thank you" that was engraved on my mind as vividly as a colorful work of art. "He bought a comforter set for me," I thought to myself. Was this a sign? Or was I just all of a sudden looking for one?

You will hear a lot of people say that at this point in a new acquaintance that this would be the beginning of many meetings or conversations to get to know one another, right? Wrong. It was just the opposite. There was only one phone call that ignited a seemingly perfect moment. It was like a paradise where only he and I existed as we engaged and indulged in our bodies, getting to know and understand the other's desires with no words being said. Even though the intimacy was full of sound, but silent of words, there was no misunderstanding of each other's desires. It was all like a fantasy, and the acquaintance was made.

Now, I have never read a love story, nor have I ever had the desire to do so. So do not expect the usual, for I do not know what that is. All I know is my story, and something keeps urging me to put it on paper. Now let's get back to my story.

It was like a fantasy, and the acquaintance was made. It was a faintly cool and dreary night, which seemed to have hidden all thoughts of concern and apprehension. It

[4]

presented itself to be the perfect night and everything was right. I hated to leave, but Momma was waiting - waiting for the clock to strike if you know what I mean. Even though there was a perfectly electrical connection by night, the daylight spoke differently. Words of shame and embarrassment filled my mind and I could no longer face him without a reduced feeling of self-respect; So I hid myself. I found it hard to be myself any longer because morally what I had done just wasn't, as the old folks say, ladylike. I concurred, but I just couldn't help it because there was just something about him that made my lips smile.....the lips between my hips, that is. I was like a carnivore that wasn't hungry enough to eat my prey, but excitingly curious enough to tastefully examine him from head to toe to keep for a later meal. Oh baby, it was like a party-for-two smorgasbord, or so I thought. But that damn daylight. Just like a wild beast I hid, not wanting to be seen by my prey for fear that he would crouch and hide at the sight of the wild one. I was embarrassed by my actions, to say the least. Daylight…I couldn't wait until dark…

It is amazing how for so long I have allowed factors around me to control the gifted person within me. Each time I started to write, something would happen that caused pain and I would stop dead in my tracks and never start back. Later, when the feeling to write would hit me again, it would be in a totally different direction, so there was never any completion. We all know what that means: No forward movement. What you have read so far was the first writing that I started when my husband and I were doing well again, after many falls, and my soul was now ready to take

[5]

its turn and speak. I was ready to reminisce about the journey he and I had through the years, but I soon came to another unexpected, unmarked curve on the road of healing and love that had no guardrail to protect me. I tumbled out of control again.

Now I know the descriptive choice of words in my first writing may be categorized by some as risqué and dangerous for sensitive ears, but that's my life and it's my story. The only way you will get the message I am about to give you is to allow yourself to see where I have been, without judging me, in order to understand where I am now. As you read along, you will continue to hear me say, "I am still growing."

I look at life so much differently now. The trials have not stopped; they are still trying to throw sucker punches at me because they are too afraid to face me head on and I am just going to keep bobbing and weaving until I knock every one of them out. I will no longer allow myself to be bullied by shame and self-pity. I only want to touch people's lives through my stories and experiences, in a positive way, and leave a positive mark everywhere I go.

Nowadays, as I go through each day, no matter what I am doing my thoughts are constantly in motion, searching for a great idea or direction in life, and this is not a bad thing at all. Sometimes allowing your thoughts to be all over the place and not controlled by one thing, as I have allowed to happen in this book, is good. Because of this, I guarantee you that everyone reading it will receive a different message that will ignite a fire so deep in you that you will start to burn inside to become the best you can be. All of us need to constructively figure out ways to keep going so that our gifts and talents are not covered up, waiting for another season to come. I no longer believe that I have to sit and wait on a season so I claim every season as my own, because every season that God created is totally different, but still positively purpose-filled for everyone.

I will no longer look at my life as a picture in a frame that cannot be changed. I will be changed inside and out and be a true example of not a risk-taker, but a faith-taker.

I am a new creature ready to spread my wings and fly.

COME AND FLY WITH ME TO A PLACE WHERE THERE IS NO ROOM FOR THE F.L.U.

A PLACE CALLED PROSPERITY.

F.L.U.

Chapter 1

F.L.U.

I was so sick. Of course I tried all of the home remedies first, using everyone else's advice but the Doctor's. The medicine just wasn't working and I was only getting worse. I finally made an appointment and took a visit to talk to the Doctor. The **F.L.U.**, like so many other illnesses, is hard to recognize at first. We always want to believe that it is just a simple condition that can get better on its own. Because we do not recognize it, it only becomes worse until it can be categorized as the **F.L.U.**: **F**AILURE of **L**IVING **U**P to your God-given potential. I had it, and it was full-blown.

Now, are you sick and tired of being more sick than tired? According to Psalms 37:23, each and every single step we take is directed by God, and He delights in every step we take, and this does not exclude prosperity. God takes joy in seeing us with financial increase and a life of happiness as we work according to His greatest command, as stated in Mathew 22:36-37, to love the Lord with all your heart, soul, and mind. With this being said, release your gifts, talents, and natural abilities and use them. They were given to us not just for sharing, but for increase. We have to understand that God equipped each and every one of us with a unique talent or gift that was strategically designed specifically for you and that can be used for prosperity as long as you understand, recognize, and acknowledge where your gift(s) and talents come from. It is alright to be a singer for God and also earn a living by using your talent as well. Now, you may think that there are a lot of people with your particular talent and feel like there is nothing to be gained from using it. Well, I can guarantee you that there is something distinctively different about you compared to everybody else with a similar gift. Please remember, God is too powerful to have to duplicate a gift. Similar - Yes! The same - No! Because of your faithfulness, God has granted you the privilege of obtaining financial prosperity.

God equipped every one of us with everything we need to be able to enjoy the fruits of life. Let me give you an example to make it easier for you to understand. God wants us to be able to enjoy our families, friends, and loved ones by worshipping together as well as vacationing together, and you have got to have money for the vacations. Understanding what the **F.L.U.** is opens the gateway to living a **F.L.U.**-free life filled with prosperity.

IDEAS/NOTE TO SELF

Do I Have The F.L.U.?

Chapter 2

DO I HAVE THE F.L.U.?

In order for you to answer this question, you have got to ask yourself another question: Am I honoring the Lord by giving Him the first part of all my income? If your answer to this is "No," then the answer to the first question is simple: You have been diagnosed with the **F.L.U.** According to Proverbs 3:9-10, we are commanded to honor the Lord by giving Him the first part of all our income and He, in return for your faithfulness, will fill your barns with wheat and barley and overflow your wine vats with the finest wines. Let's relate this to today. Accept the fact that God will fill your life with the best because of your faithfulness and obedience.

Now having said that let me start by saying this: I have been battling the effect of going back and forth for a long time. I am applying the Word to my life daily, but this has not been happening for very long. I am growing daily and seeing things from a much different perspective now. But I must say this to you: I am a 44 year old baby girl of God crawling and starting to show signs of being able to walk, but only with my Father holding my hand. Remember, I am still growing.

my cup has a leak

In my recent growth I have come to realize that because of my disobedience in my tithing, my financial growth is an inflated reflection of my giving.

four positions available and i didn't get one of them; another bad news distraction.

keep writing karen, keep writing.

Even though I give a little, God so graciously gives a lot in return. He really does way too much as it relates to my giving. Because God loves me, He allows my existence to continue on a level that is better than barely surviving, which would represent the real reflection of my giving, but it is still like a cup with an open bottom. God is the most honorable loan officer any of us will ever know. He is the easiest person to borrow from, and the one that I have owed the longest, but yet I still put him behind every other bill collector. He only asks for ten percent. His payment plan is very flexible. If you make $200.00, it's ten percent. If you make $20.00, it's still only ten percent. Unlike other loan institutions, He will never keep the payments high when your money gets low. Just ten percent!

[14]

which way did it go?

I know at this point that many of you can relate to this part of my life. I have been on the winning end financially in the past, but where did it go? What did I do wrong? What did I just not do? I went from almost debt-free to a debt disease. After I examined my questions, I quickly discovered that I had lost sight of who actually made everything play out in perfect order for my financial increase. I forgot that the receipt that I possessed for payment of my Grace and Mercy was signed by the blood of Jesus! I had started to place the need for continued financial success ahead of God himself. I had started working every Sunday and using that as a false reason for not attending church regularly anymore. I worked all during the week and did not give of my time or tithe anymore, and had totally lost my understanding of the value of my true existence. Am I where I should be? No, but I am working my way back. But once again, as I will continue to say, I am still growing, and I can truly see the difference even as I write these words. Take this opportunity to grow with me by remembering the words of Paul, "I am still not all I should be but I am bringing all my energies to bear on this one thing; forgetting about the past and looking forward to what it is that lies ahead." Your blessing may be in the lost and found section of your spirit, but it has your name on it and is waiting to be reconnected with you. If you are limiting your faith, STOP! Start wearing your own personal message: "WARNING: A BREAK-THROUGH IS ON THE WAY!" Think about

[15]

prosperity this way: According to Exodus 33, the Lord told Moses to lead his people to a land flowing with milk and honey that He had promised to Abraham, Isaac, and Jacob. Now put on your thinking cap and ponder this - if you put milk and honey together, what do you get? MONEY!

IDEAS/NOTE TO SELF

I Knew I had the F.L.U. but Didn't Know What to do

Chapter 3

I KNEW I HAD THE F.L.U. BUT DIDN'T KNOW WHAT TO DO

Even though I understood all of the recommendations that were given to me by the Doctor for ridding myself of the **F.L.U.**, I was not ready to jump right in. The human side of me was not ready to clean out my closet of all my old ways of seeing and doing things. I looked at several scriptures to try to come to grips with this psychological dilemma that I had suddenly thrown myself into. As I read, there was one thing that stood out to me and made a strong impression upon my heart. It was 2 Corinthians 8:9, in which Paul tells us that the Lord was so full of love for us that even though He was rich, He became very poor so that His poorness would make us rich. I suddenly understood how much He loved me. The Lord's love was filled with sacrifices that He made so that we could reap the benefits of an awesome life of prosperity and wealth by using our gifts and talents.

what to do

At this moment, my mind was still questioning what to do. Then I remembered that God does not start any work that He will not complete, and that is when I decided to use what He had given me. I started using every talent, gift, natural ability, or whatever you want to call it, that was in me. We can't just pray about success; we have got to do something about it. Use your talents! Use your gifts! Spiritually recognize and understand them so that they can be used in the most powerful way that will reach someone in need and bring you the financial prosperity you deserve. How can we continue to fail an open book test when all of the answers have been given to us in one book? God did not mandate that we suffer financially. His favor allows us to share in his wealth.

Understanding this can help you differentiate between your talents and gifts to help enlighten your spiritual knowledge even more. A talent means having a great ability, knack, or expertise in something. A gift means to be given an endowment of something; to permanently possess something of value. Endowments usually come in the form of the giving of things of great value for a person to build wealth from. The difference between your talent and your gift is this: Your talent can move you in a forward motion and sustain you, but your gift is what will empower you to gain the riches mandated for you. A talent will get you there, but it takes a gift to keep you there! Use it!

It is no mistake that we are awakened in the wee hours of the night, and our thoughts go directly to what I call "spiritual growing pains." We immediately think about our life and its uncertainties, or "lifestances" as I call them, that we are facing that are causing us pain. At this moment, you should ask the Lord to give you comfort about these things, and give you discernment to understand and direction to remove them from your life, so that the door to prosperity can open freely. Do you want to come in?

who's Calling?

In order for God to communicate with us one on one, He will sometimes give us these wake-up calls to speak to us before the alarm clocks sounds, which starts the day-to-day rat race that we call life. My spiritual phone call usually comes through about 4:44 a.m. Start paying attention and listen for your call from God. He has given us a lifetime supply of Mercy and Grace that allows us to continually blossom, even with the misfires of life that we call mistakes. His one-on-one communication with us will allow us to grow with strength and wisdom, gain with knowledge and wealth, and give with love. I call it the 3 G's: GROW, GAIN, and GIVE. The 3 G's create a positive, optimistic spirit that will kill the "crab in the bucket" attitude of keeping others down and cause you to want to bring others into this lifestyle of living prosperously through Christ.

As I think about how hard it is for me to get the attention of a wealthy person and to get them to have a serious conversation with me about my ideas and writings, I have discovered that they, many times unknowingly, exhibit a crab mentality by simply negating the value of someone who may not be a part of their social or financial status, thus far making their chance for success, based on a great idea, slim to none. If you don't believe me, think about one of your favorite reality shows and how they put thousands of dollars into some of the most idiotic ideas and make them work. Would they have put that type of trust, money, and effort into my idea? Never in a million years. Getting their attention is about as hard as a slave asking his master for his freedom papers. Seems like a subtle form of discrimination based on financial status: me not being worth enough for the risk. Another crab in the bucket. Lord, send a wealthy angel my way; I have so much to share.

Interactions

Did you know that we can sometimes tap into our talents and gifts through our interactions with others? Try thinking back to interacting with employees, employers, family, friends, strangers, etc. and remember what events, words, or circumstances peaked your interest the most while interacting with them. This will give you some needed insight to help you identify your talents and your gifts that will equip you to fight the **F.L.U.**, and will begin the immunization process of protecting your very soul from the **F.L.U.**

One of the many gifts that I have recognized in myself is the gift of elderly companionship. I never knew this until I worked in a senior citizen environment. I should have recognized it years before, because even at a young age I was always drawn to my elders. I even joined the church senior choir at about the age of 25. Another gift that I have is the gift of words, whether it is for advice, reasoning,

[22]

understanding, encouragement or just a laugh. Regardless of where I am personally, I find comfort in being able to help someone who is experiencing down times in life dealing with work, finances, relationships, acceptance issues, and other dilemmas of life.

There is one other ability I possess that I am careful about revealing, because when people just aren't ready for certain levels of spirituality, they classify you as crazy. However, because I want to help at least one person believe in God-given gifts, talents and signs to help him or her let go and let God, here it is: Since I was a little girl things have been revealed to me in dreams and visions. I cannot tell you exactly how old I was, but before my grandmother's death, I can remember that when things were bothering me, I would have a dream of three tornados in one. Since I was very close to my grandmother, she was the only one I told about this. Even though I did not tell her that something felt wrong, she told me that dreams of tornados meant that whatever storm I was going through was about to end. Now, being around the age of eleven, what could possibly be going wrong? It was very soon after this that my grandmother, my idol, my heart, was taken away from me. Even though it was many years later before I had another tornado dream, I always remembered what she told me, and she was absolutely right. Whenever there was overwhelming trouble in my marriage or with my children, there was the dream, and soon afterwards, the relief. Staying on the subject of dreams, I dreamed of two of my children before they were born. In March of 1988, I had a dream that I was in labor having a baby. In the dream I gave birth to a light-skinned baby girl with a long head full of nappy hair. Guess what? About two weeks later, I gave birth to a light-skinned baby girl with a long head and nappy hair (lol). The long head soon disappeared because her head was actually stretched from suction. I also dreamed about my middle child's birth and saw a baby boy in the dream but I thought to myself, "This is just a coincidence." Surprise! I had a baby boy, who was born 3 months premature a couple of weeks later. It was so funny because my water actually broke while I had my daughter sitting between my legs combing her hair, and she took off running and told my mother that I had peed on her neck. All joking aside: Even though all births are miracles, my middle child was definitely a miracle child, as the doctor had only given him until morning to live. Thank God for a praying mother! My mother stayed right there by my bedside and said boldly, "We are not claiming this!" She said a very quick and to-the-point prayer: "Lord, if you let him live, I promise I will never whip him." Well, when he was about the age of two, she went back to God to ask if she could take that promise back, because he had become a roaring, rambunctious toddler.

My visions began a few years later into motherhood, and so far have only related to my children or close family. The first time was when I was attending evening church service. While I was sitting there listening to the preacher deliver his message, I suddenly saw my daughter being burned or on fire in the kitchen of my parent's home. A feeling of fear hit me so intensely that I had to leave church to go and make a phone call to check on her. When my niece

[24]

answered the phone, I immediately asked where my daughter was. She told me that she was in the kitchen cooking. I told her "Go and stop her right now!" I said it over and over again. The tension I was feeling quickly came to a halt. Thank God for this vision that saved my daughter's life. And just think, He allowed me to see this even though at this time in my life, church for me was just tradition and not spiritual; or so I thought. He still used me as a vessel. There was also a vision I received while I was sitting working quietly at my desk one day. Even though it was only for a split second, as they usually were, I saw my daughter leaving out of the school doors and getting into a car in the parking lot of her school. Because so many years had passed since I had a vision, I just shook it off. A couple of days later, on a whim, I decide to take off from work early and meet her at the bus stop so that we could go and do something together. The bus came and left and there was no sign of my daughter. Even though she was just a sophomore, she had skipped school to go on what's called "senior skip day." I did not see me beating her in the vision, but if it were not for my dad, oh boy! But she did get a pretty good work over from me and my mom. It was a tag team match made for pay-per-view. My latest vision occurred when my son was accused of fathering a child with a young lady. We went through months of waiting and accusations from the girl's family, but I wanted to do everything the right way: DNA. We sat quietly by, letting the blows come. Before the child was born, I had told my daughter that I wasn't sure if I was dreaming or not, but I saw a DNA test that showed that he was not the father.

Soon afterwards, the child was born and the test was taken. 98.9% he was not the father. Thank God for giving me visions as one of the many free protection plans he has for me and my family.

have you discovered yours?

Take a moment to pause and think about it. Have you discovered your gifts and talents? Identifying your gifts and talents is crucial. I am reminded of one of my sisters, who to this day, has the power of persuasion. I remember one day when we were children, about five of us were playing tag in our back yard. Well, my athletically-gifted brother was running from a friend of ours and ran up a mulberry tree. At this point, being that this tree was taller than our house, our friend did not realize how high he had climbed to catch my brother until it was too late. Just as fast as my brother climbed up the tree, he climbed down. Unfortunately, this was not the case for our friend. No one could talk him down as he hung onto a limb so tightly that it looked like a third leg. I ran into the house to get my older sister and I told her that our friend was in the tree and was too scared to come down. Now, even though I sounded afraid and a little hysterical, she didn't flinch or rush to check for that matter, as she was sipping her Kool-Aid from a wine glass watching the "Big Show." As a matter of fact, I don't even remember her moving until a commercial break. After a few minutes, while still sipping from her wine glass of Kool-Aid, she came outside and observed. She then sent one of us in the house to get a blanket. She looked at all four of us and instructed everybody to grab a corner of the blanket and hold it tightly. She then looked up at our friend and with a strong persuasive voice she told him to jump when she counted to three. She counted; no jump. He started crying saying he was too scared to jump. She took another sip of Kool-Aid from her wine glass, with her pinky finger out, and told everybody to drop the blanket and leave him up there. As he cried out to us not to leave him, she told him that she was going to count again and he had better jump. In a much softer voice of persuasion that carried in the wind like an angel, she said, "They gonna catch ya." With that being said, the flight of horror began. On her last

a necessary distraction for laughter; keep writing karen, keep writing.

command, he jumped. Now, even though it only took a couple of seconds for him to fall, it looked like time had slowed down to almost motionless. As he jumped, with his arms spread out wide, his 150 pounds looked like a 210 pound flying squirrel. My sister screamed, "Drop the

[27]

blanket!" and we did. He hit the ground like a falling tree. We all looked in silence and horror while his brother stated the obvious, "You done killed my brother." Now my sister, with the usual smirk she was known for, responded very confidently, "He alright." In what seemed like an hour but was actually closer to five seconds, he jumped up from the ground and took off running home. My brother turned to my sister and asked her, "Why did you tell us to let the blanket go?" She laughed and said, "Boy, he woulda broke all y'all arms." She always had, and still does have, the power of persuasion to make what appears to be impossible seem possible. Use your gifts and talents!

bite your tongue

Remembering that life and death are in the power of the tongue, speak only great things about yourself. Our power is in the gifts that God has given us from birth. There is a saying that children are like sponges and you can teach them anything. As parents, we have got to focus not only on our talents and gifts, but on our children's talents and gifts as well so that they will not become sufferers of the **F.L.U.** Stop blaming all of their traits on genetics and start being conscious of the messages that our words, activities, actions, and non-actions are sending out, because we are passing these acquired traits on to our children. Even more importantly, we need to stop telling ourselves and our children negative things. Put it this way: Just because Momma or Daddy has a temper does not justify you allowing that child to have a temper that leads him or her to

[28]

great troubles. Discover the goodness and gifts in that child and allow that child to dream, and I guarantee you that the talents and gifts will then start to sprout up, grow, and be ready for use. They will override any anger trait that he or she has picked up from a parent. WARNING! Most dream blockers are usually those that are closest to you. For yourself and those you are around, remember this: Most of our dreams are created around our gifts and talents. Dreams reveal the secret hiding places of our gifts. STOP DREAMING! MAKE IT REAL!

buried treasures

Search out your talents and gifts if you have lost sight of them. Think back to when you were a child. You had no fear of singing, writing, building, talking or whatever it was you loved doing. But as we grow older and allow outside elements like acceptance and premature adult responsibilities to cause worry, we allow the gifts and talents to become buried so deep that we lose them. The great thing about this is, just as lost cities and treasures can be found thousands of years later and be worth more than they were when they were created, so can your gifts and talents be found, renewed, and revived. Their value will be immeasurable. Remember, you are a living treasure just waiting to be opened. Be on your way to great discoveries that are just waiting to bless your life. For the sake of yourself and your family, make the decision to be healed and not even allow yourself to be a carrier of failure.

he's taking a what?

Get out of the habit of "taking a break" from God. You may not say it that way, but I will be the first to admit that I will sometimes get up on a Sunday morning looking for an excuse not to make it to church. But what if He decided, even for one second, to take a break from me? My existence could vanish just that quickly because God decided to get Himself an extra wink and sleep in on me.

IDEAS/NOTE TO SELF

Can You Have the F.L.U. Without Visible Signs?

Chapter 4

CAN YOU HAVE THE F.L.U. WITHOUT VISIBLE SIGNS?

The answer is definitely "yes." I Timothy 6:10 says to us that the love of money is the first step toward all types of sin. Many of us have, knowingly and unknowingly, turned away from God because of our love of money. With this being said, a person consumed by money and having lots of it will sometimes not recognize that they are sick with the **F.L.U.** because there are no physical financial signs of sickness or suffering. They feel on top of the world because of their money. What is even sadder, many of the people around them feel that this type of person is a representation of true success, not realizing their wealth is being temporarily supplied by the God they have deserted.

i wish i could be as relaxed as my dog laying here with no worries.

keep writing karen, keep writing.

Please understand, the means which some of them have used to get this money is not important to them at all. They have been blinded by their love of money.

come on guys

Today, drugs and promiscuous lifestyles have laid claim to many of our young brothers and sisters, with no cultural or racial boundaries. They are falling by the wayside for the love of money. The O'Jays wrote a song called "For the Love of Money." The song speaks of what happens when this illusion of love takes control of a person and causes a man to rob his mother, and a woman to sell her body. Even though they are living a life of darkness, they do not recognize they are not living up to their God-given potential, because they can afford to soothe all of their desires for material things. Take a minute to think about the people you may know that are living their lives in a way that is totally against what God wants from them. Here you are, trying to live right, but they seem to have all the financial prosperity. Just keep in mind, since they have completely eliminated God from their lifestyle, their souls are slowing decaying away and their prosperity is only temporary and will quickly lead to poverty, destruction, and death. If a person like this stopped and reevaluated themselves by looking at his or her life as a successful business, they would have to evaluate the tools and means used to achieve that level of success and then determine if the measures will eventually be destructive to their business. Once this question is examined they will find that the answer is yes, and a restructuring of the business (body) for positive growth is crucial or the business (body) will fail completely.

it's dark

I was once a person who had the **F.L.U.** with no visible signs. I can remember so well how, back in 2005, my family was struggling so badly that every bill we had was past due; everything, including our home, was in trouble. I was so tired of not being able to sleep at night, and had started turning my phone off because we couldn't even relax after working all day for the phone ringing with bill collectors threatening to take what was theirs. No matter how much I opened up the blinds throughout the house to let the sunshine in, to me it was still very dark inside. We were at risk of losing everything. Living paycheck to paycheck had become the norm, but it was never comfortable. Asking my family for money had over stayed its welcome. My older brother gave for the last time before finally refusing. He told me that I needed to let my husband figure it out. I then sat down with my husband one day, and I told him that he had to do something because we just couldn't keep going like this. His job was not paying enough to keep our heads above water. Now, I was also employed, but I really felt that at this point it was his place to be the provider and step up in times like this. Well anyway, after telling him that he needed to do something differently, he told me that he was happy with what he was doing. Now, this really blew my mind because I just could not fathom how someone could be happy doing anything that could not support his family. To help you better understand the situation, let me take you back a little further to show you how this could actually be possible. Whenever that desperate measure was needed to make something happen financially, usually to keep us with transportation and a house, I took what I thought were the necessary steps to make it happen. Some of the steps I am not proud of, but I did it for my family. All he knew was that whatever was pressing had been taken care of, and he could continue to sleep at night very well, just as he had when it wasn't taken care of. He never questioned how the money magically appeared. At this time, I was working as a property manager and was earning more money than my husband, but I was still asking God for a way to do better. A few days later, early in the morning before daybreak, as usual, as soon as I opened my eyes, I saw myself with a cleaning service. Just as quickly as the vision happened, the name of the business came out of my mouth. That day, I immediately started to take action. A couple of months later, I was ready to take that leap of faith and step away from my daytime job to pursue being a full-time entrepreneur. After completely preparing to leave my full-time job, fear kicked in and I started changing my mind. There were no on-the-job problems and I was in control of everything. Well, when God speaks, He has a strong way of making you listen. Immediately, all hell broke loose on my job. "Ok Lord," was my response, and I was out of there. I took the $4200.00, which was all I had in a small retirement account, and set out, fully equipped by Faith, to go into business as a cleaning service provider. After getting all of the business expenses taken care of, I took $98.00 to buy cleaning supplies and I hit the pavement running. My first contract was with a major company, providing them with new construction cleaning of an exclusive apartment complex with over two hundred units. Wow! I was so proud of myself for being able to land such a deal, but then the fear of failure kicked in. Even though I had no funds to pay anybody to help me, and my husband was not on board with working what he considered two jobs, God was on board. He sent my brothers, my sister, sister-in-law, brother-in-law, my children, and my mother to help me start out. We worked late into the night. But the support from home just wasn't there. With calluses on my hands, even though I wanted to be a woman, my husband's actions insisted that I be a man. My family worked with me even after working a full-time job all day long, and never asked me for a dime and never complained; well not to me, that is. They worked with me to meet whatever deadline I had, and stayed with me until I was able to cash my first few checks and pay someone to work with me. Thank God for strength and sacrifice from my family, and thank God for my mother who wouldn't let them tell me "no" anyway. Now to make an even longer story short, I continued to do very well and started giving myself all the credit for my success. We were living more comfortably than we ever had before, and now I thought that money was the key to our happiness. As I continued to enable my husband by stepping in to wear his pants for the protection and provisions of our family, I did not realize that cleaning was a talent that God allowed me to use to get on my feet so that I could pursue my dreams through the gifts He had given me. I knew in my spirit that my cleaning service was temporary, because it had been revealed long before, and the knowing had been stirring around in me from the beginning. I just didn't understand due to the obscurity of the feeling, so I just worked harder at getting new businesses when that was not what God was trying to tell me at all. Needless to say, the business just would not grow anymore, and started to steadily decrease. I was sick and blinded by what I thought could only bring true happiness: money. God will accept taking a back seat for a while, but anything gained in vain will go straight down the drain. Know exactly what it is you want before you go asking for something. I should have asked God for discernment, but I did not know then what I know now. But as I keep saying, I am still growing.

Now please do not judge the person who I chose to be my husband, because I do accept responsibility in the role that I played in controlling his actions. God made me a very strong woman with purpose. The problem stemmed from me not allowing God to lead me in the use of my strength, which simply means I was using it in the wrong way, and this ultimately turned my strength into a weakness. By listening to the devil, many times through the mouths of others, my strength caused me to walk into territory that my feet weren't made to travel. The more I tried to take control, the more everything unraveled. Rather than letting the chips fall where they may, I had completely changed the direction of growth my husband very well could have and would have taken if I had just refrained from always taking control of every situation. As a family, all the women in my family are known for being women of strength. I had to point this out to my daughter so that she would not do the same thing in her relationship, because I could already see it manifesting in the same direction. She later told me she saw exactly what I meant and she would not allow it to continue.

boys to men

Let me say this to mothers (hello self) and fathers, just as a note of advice: Make your boys into men before they leave your home. Since parenthood does not come with instructions we all make mistakes with it. After I realized mine, I developed a list called "Things you should know before you go." Even though the list is not very long, it holds a very strong message: Get your own and keep your own.

Things You Should Know Before You Go

Savings & Credit: Don't be obsessed with riding large and living large on a servant's pay. Plan out your life with goals of where you want to be one, five, and ten years from now, and keep your credit clean. Get enough to start building your score, but not so much to find yourself swimming in debt.

Emergency Fund: When starting out, save, save, save. Periodically treat yourself to something special to appreciate yourself for your hard work and dedication to saving, but not too expensive. When an emergency arises, you will be financially well-prepared and able to sustain yourself without falling into debt because of the unexpected, like most of us have done.

Insurance: Teach him the importance of insurance in all areas, whether it be vehicle, property, life, dental, or health. They need to budget this into their financial pyramid early. Just because your parents can cover you with their medical insurance until you are twenty six does not mean they want to.

Household utilities and other household expenses: Every young man should be taught this early. They really think they can do it easily, and do not understand the percentage of their income that will be taken when they rush to move out on their own without having a monthly budget plan established. They fall into debt because of lack of preparation and are back home before you know it, and usually with more issues than what they left with.

Dress for Success: Dress for the job you want, not necessarily the job you are applying for or have. Dress for increase. When the right people see you, the right things will happen for you. Since we never know when or where that will be, we always have to present ourselves in a manner of expecting increase. First impressions have caused many young men to get left behind. Even though he is a dependable, hard-working individual, this is not the person who was seen at the first meeting. His first impression was suffocated by the image of his negatively put-together attire. Opportunity immediately disappears. The first impression is the master of impressions. Most of the time, it is the only impression with no second chance. I truly believe that any grown man that is of the age of twenty or older that continues to wear his pants below his waistline has mentally stopped maturing. Always remember I Corinthians 13:11, "When I was a child, I spoke as a child, I understood as a child, I thought as a child, but when I became a man, I put away childish things." Do this and grow up! Make your image one that demands respect and reflects success. STOP CREATING OBSTACLES FOR YOURSELF!

God: Definitely not the least: GOD. Teach him the power he holds as a man according to the Word. Teach him his place in a marriage and his family will not fail or suffer. These instructions are not brain breakers; they are quite simple if we would only read them. (As a note: many of these rules can apply to daughters too.) Now continuing… Don't send your son off to become a son of his wife. Teach him how to love himself. Make sure he understands what the Bible says about marriage before he says "I do." Let him know that he is taking the step towards loving his wife as Christ loved the church.

Yes, I know we live in a day where women are able to do everything that a man does, but guess what, I don't want to do everything a man does. If God wanted one to be able to do everything the other does, he would not have created two. Don't get me wrong, the movement for women's rights has done many great things for women, but let's keep it real. If our features were like a man's there would be no intimacy for procreation. Human life would become extinct. So let a man be a man! A wife cannot do it like her husband, but she can help him command his fort, and stand by and defend him through the ups and downs. Needless to say, speaking from personal experience, by continuing to enable my husband I tried to lead my home and literally worked like a slave in the process. So to my sister wives, get that monkey off your back! If the husband allows the woman to lead the home, his marriage and his home will surely fail. When a man finds a wife he finds a good thing, so men, put a padlock on it. If you have problems in the home, don't let her go through them alone. Become a team, and you the team leader. Start searching immediately when you see that her happiness is beginning to slip away. Lastly, when enough is enough and you ask him to leave, don't allow him to come back just as he left. Welcome in the MAN OF THE HOUSE THAT IS READY TO TAKE HIS PLACE ACCORDING TO THE WORD - It worked for me, and it can work for you. But remember, you have to allow your man to finally meet the love-filled woman given to him by God and you MUST now operate in that manner. Stop the verbal disrespect of the word "submit" when the word is what actually protects us from being misused, abused and neglected from our true needs and wants. LET HIM SEE HIS TRUE QUEEN!

If you are unsure if he really loves you, say this to yourself and listen as you speak, and your question will be answered: "I know what love is and what love does not do." If he is still doing what love does not do, you have your answer. And ladies, please don't read more into this than what has been said. If you need more clarification, go to the Word or your spiritual advisor. This is only my statement, and as I told you before, I am still growing.

ahhh my battery died on me; thank God for

auto-save; a necessary distraction,

keep writing karen, keep writing

you go, girl!

To my sisters: there are some of us that talk the talk, and admire others that walk the walk, but have trouble walking towards success ourselves. They have mastered encouraging others, but have mentally enslaved themselves into thinking they are incapable of being successful, when just being a woman is a perfect representation of success itself. They will say things that deep down inside they do not believe. They only say these things to justify where they are in life; also known as EXCUSES. Start taking new steps in life by no longer allowing yourself, particularly your body, to be used for money. Some of the best pole dancers, who have settled for being strippers in a club, allowing their bodies to be raped by the eyes, and many times, hands of both men and women, could have been some of the greatest, highest paid gymnasts and most graceful praise dancers. I will be the first to say it takes true skills, talent, and upper body strength to be able to hold your own body's weight and perform as elegantly as they do. Come on ladies, be encouraged and make the choice to use your gift in the right way.

Just a note to fathers and stepfathers, treat your daughters like the princesses they are, and that image that is driven into their head by their fathers will not allow negative men to enter their lives. Therefore, no other man will be able to tell her anything less than the best. My dad calls all of his daughters his darling, and he makes each one of us feel individually special, as if each of us is his favorite. I did not find this out until I was about forty years old and my oldest sister surprisingly showed up from North Carolina and she yelled, "Daddy!" and he returned the excitement with a voice of jubilance, "There go my baby!" Right then, both of them looked like frogs to me. I was so mad I could have just fallen over and played dead like a possum. Up until this point, I really was naively thinking that I was the favorite of all his daughters, which was quite selfish on my part. With all jokes aside, I never knew that he took the time to create special moments with each of us that would make me and my sisters feel equally as his favorite. There was something inside of me that just really wanted to say that. Thanks, Dad!

IDEAS/NOTE TO SELF

How Can I Make Myself Immune From the F.L.U.?

Chapter 5

HOW CAN I MAKE MYSELF IMMUNE FROM THE F.L.U.?

According to I Timothy 4:8, physical exercise is good, but spiritual exercise is much more important and is a tonic for all you do. It will not only help you now, but it will also help you in the life to come. Do this with sound doctrine and you will be equipped with the power to live, grow, and prosper. We all remember the song we sang in vacation bible school: "The B-I-B-L-E, that's the book for me." Oh, the frowns that came along with singing it, because we had to sing before we could eat or play. Oh, the days! As I got older I realized that the words to the song, even though they were few, were powerful: TO STAND ALONE ON THE WORD OF GOD. Find a way to constantly remind yourself to read and pray.

The prayer reminder that I found to be good for me was the thought of my kids. Anytime one of them came to mind, I started immediately saying "Thank you, Lord," and repeating the word protection three times. When I started doing this, I found that I thought of my kids more than 30 to 40 times a day that I could consciously recall. Wow! And just think about the fact that I am God's baby girl and He thinks of me more than I think about my own children. He has more responsibilities to me than I will ever have with my own children, because He put all of His promises to me in writing and signed them with His blood.

Remember, being perfect and completely spirit-filled is not a requirement to be a player on His team. I now understand that He is waiting on a sometimes stubborn, slip-of-the tongue curser like me. And yes! I am still growing. And yes! I am on His team. I may be on the sideline learning the game, but guess what, I am going to claim my first string position!

Challenge!!!

Challenge yourself. Having heard that if you do something for 21 days it will likely become a habit, caused me to challenge myself to read the Bible, since I only read for informational purposes. I really despised reading. I decided to read a verse, chapter, or whatever I chose from the Bible daily for 21 days. And to my surprise, I made an amazing discovery. The 21-day challenge worked for me.

the mechanic says the car is ready to be picked up and when he gets there the car won't crank up
keep writing karen, keep writing

First of all, when I got to the 21st day I didn't realize it because I was no longer having the urge to count the days. By this time I was reading twice daily, at least two to three chapters a day, and was eager to do so. It had become a habit, and it was on!

I challenge you to read the Bible daily for 21 days. It will be the most beautiful love story you will ever read. If you don't know exactly where to start reading, my advice would be to start with the book of Proverbs. Most people can really understand and relate to the book of Proverbs and it will probably make you say "ouch" right from the beginning. It will reveal to you some of the very same things that we are dealing with today. You will learn about things like vouching for someone's credit, hard work and prosperity, self-control and the lack thereof, how wise people think ahead, two sides to every story, a lazy man going hungry, what happens when you refuse to admit to your mistakes, what wisdom gives us, staying away from prostitutes, selfishness, and so many other things that we encounter and interact with in our everyday living. Proverbs hits directly at the pit of your stomach, verse after verse, like a boxer (GOD) winning the fight with a mighty combination of punches and ending with a TKO. You will definitely be more careful about every step you take, words you say, and decisions you make. I call Proverbs the book of the Bible for dummies. If you are a beginner, like me, I recommend using a Bible that is easy for you to understand. I guarantee you will begin to change your way of thinking, which will change your way of believing, which will ultimately change your way of doing. Your strength will be renewed and you will be eager to stay in a healthy spiritual state of mind and make yourself immune to the **F.L.U.** Remember, the Word is the only thing that is the same yesterday, today, and forever. All other forms of information are apt to change. Any other advice will be good for you today, but five years later will kill you. The Word will always be the same. In my opinion, there are only two permanent things, and those are change and the Word. Now, don't be stupid like me and let your actions test the Word and sign you up for a bunch of rematches. You'll get knocked out every time. I am not telling you what I heard; I'm telling you what I have learned. And remember, I am still growing!

IDEAS/NOTE TO SELF

Can the F.L.U. be Seasonal?

Chapter 6

CAN THE F.L.U. BE SEASONAL?

Yes, definitely so. Weeping may endure for a night, but joy comes in the morning. So when I get up in the morning, my first words are, "Thank you Lord and Good morning Joy.

phone message: i am a debt collector and this is an attempt to collect a debt blah blah blah a seasonal distraction. keep writing karen, keep writing.

This passage comes from Psalms 30:5, which also tells us that His anger lasts a moment but His favor lasts for a lifetime. Spiritually, we allow ourselves to go up and down emotionally like a roller coaster. One of the primary causes is that God allows us to absorb and find comfort in enjoying the benefits of health, wealth, and other fulfillments of life but we then lose sight of God, who signs our paychecks and prescriptions. We get above ourselves and lose sight of the true prize of Salvation. When this happens, your cup will become low again, but the good

[53]

news is you can get a refill for a spill. He will fill us up again to start over. We should use the Bible like we use a syringe filled with medicine that we quickly run to the doctor for to slow down the discomfort of the illness until it is gone. If you constantly continue exercising your mind with the Word of God, you will have a sure-fire weapon for fighting off seasonal **F.L.U.**

Begin going to Him all the time joyfully, and not in a sad state as we most often do. Go with a spirit of expectation of receiving what you need, and even your wants. Remember Malachi 3:10, "Bring all the tithes into the storehouse, that there may be food in My house, and try me now in this, says the Lord of hosts, if I will not open for you the windows of heaven and pour out for you such blessing that there will not be room enough for you to receive it." We must wake up every morning, expecting each day to be greater than the other, saying, "Good morning, Joy!"

why me? why not me!

keep writing karen, keep writing.

[54]

what did you expect?

Expectation is a necessity. God gave each of us a spirit that commands expectation of things, because if we never expected something, we wouldn't continue to work at anything. Just as we can so easily believe that bad things can happen without warning, we have got to believe and expect that great things can happen without warning.

To only desire something that you would love to have is evidence of what I consider to be a fragile and weak personality. The only effort put forth towards what you desire requires only a minimal amount of wishing, which requires less than a baby's amount of thinking. There is no oomph to get up and work towards anything. To be honest about it, a baby puts forth more effort when they desire to be fed because they will exert all of their energy to get it. You can never desire it enough to go after it. You need to stop limiting yourself and understand how success is a reflection of action. It is a positive energy that is constantly in motion, never really having an ending. You will succeed at one thing, and move on to another. You are constantly motivated to find different avenues you can take to add to what is produced from the use of your gifts and talents. Remember, small minds only see things as they are and where they are. Great minds see the hidden potential of what something can be and how far it can go. So don't just think about what makes you happy and settle for less, make it happen!

[55]

If we really truly think about our future, it will make us more accountable for today. You need to start writing things down in open, obvious places so that you will have them in front of you constantly and not forget about them; hindering you from achieving your goals and dreams. We have got to stop letting our dreams and determination take seasonal breaks.

Just thinking back, I realized that many families, including mine, have forfeited bringing their dreams into reality because of financial strains, family, work problems and so many other distractions. Some even categorize it as familial or generational curses. THIS IS NOT THE CASE! What we have become accustom to is always verbally sharing our dreams with our children but, because of life's distractions, we never allow them to see these dreams manifest into reality. They never get to witness the fruit gained from the dream becoming reality or taste the sweetness of it. Therefore, the cycle is repeated, sometimes generation after generation, because all we have taught them is how to dream and not the fruition of making a dream real. Now the result is that they are just teaching their children to dream and recreating what they learned from their parents. This also explains why some families just "have it" as we may sometimes say. It is only because someone went beyond dreaming and allowed their children the pleasure of witnessing it all. Now these children turn into adults that not only talk about it but diligently work towards making a dream come true. They understand the importance of completion as it relates to success. You cannot have one without the other. This is what I want for my family and what I am persistently working towards.

I am back in the work force right now and am no longer the boss. Working a job I simply do not like because of so much unnecessary stress and confusion but I work like it is my company. I work with an attitude that allows me to feel proud about what my work says about me at the end of the day. Am I overworked because of my work ethics? ABSOLUTELY! However, I know that this is a part of my growth to go higher and gain more than this job can ever give me. I know I can make more money than they will ever pay me by keeping myself focused on where I am going and not where I am right now. Keep your eyes on the prize, because if you can see it you can believe it, and if you believe it you can definitely achieve it. I am a living witness that can attest to the fact that you can get back up!

Just thinking back, I can recall on more than one occasion, how someone would say to me, "I always thought you were rich." Let's evaluate this. I grew up in a low-income neighborhood, hardly ever had my hair professionally done, never had my nails done, wasn't known for wearing all the name-brand clothing, shoes and purses, only drove average cars and most of them were used vehicles. As I thought about this, I could not believe what was revealed to me on the projector of my mind. I saw the person that others saw. God had given me the aura to fit the life that I should be living based upon the gifts He had given me. We need to start ordering our lives like we order our fries. LORD,

MAKE MINE A LARGE! Success can be as simple as a thought. And remember, I am still growing!

IDEAS/NOTE TO SELF

Is the F.L.U. Contagious?

Chapter 7

IS THE F.L.U. CONTAGIOUS?

Absolutely! I Corinthians 15:33 tells us to not be misled; bad company corrupts good character. You will end up just like the company you keep. Being around negative, corrupt people causes a person with 20/20 eyesight to become spiritually blind and miss out on opportunities. Your vision will become impaired to such an extent that you won't even see far enough ahead to prepare for the rewards God has in store for you through the use of your gifts and talents. You only see a closed door which is the reflection of your closed mind and the closed minds of those you are around. If you love someone that seems to be comfortable with going nowhere, you need to reevaluate yourself and determine if it is love, lust, or just plain ludicrous.

mom needs me to call her important; called; what about the roast for tomorrow's dinner?.....
      keep writing karen, keep writing

It amazes me how hundreds can stand in line at a gun show to stock up on weapons, for fear that the government is going to make some changes to control the sale of guns, but you can't get ten of us (ouch) to line up and wait for the church to open to stock up on the Word, for fear of God's return when we know He is coming like a thief in the night with no warning.

leave the light on

Close your eyes and mentally visualize a house that is totally dark inside and try to make your way to the only light you see in the house, which is the light illuminating around the edge of a closed door. This is what happens when we let what I call "lifestances" cause us to get sidetracked and bury our talents and gifts. The joy of this is that, because God is a forgiving God, He still keeps the light on, expecting your arrival at any time. The door can be opened so that you can bathe in the full flow of light that will penetrate and saturate you again for a spiritual renewal, reopening the hidden treasures.

get away

Understanding that tradition does not save us, sometimes separation is good when it allows you to let the "old you" go and make the "new you" grow. Sometimes, those that are closest to you are the last ones to realize there is change in you, and the first ones the devil will try to use against you. For whatever reason, it takes them longer to accept the change as being permanent. There are even times in our lives when we have to pull away from companions and family for a while. Because negativity will sometimes show itself around those you love the most, go the other way; make a U-turn or whatever it takes to stay away and not become consumed by it.

This reminds me of a time when one of my brothers and I got into a terribly heated argument; never experienced anything like it before in my life. There were things that were said and done to me by him that crushed me inside and out. The most vivid memory was his touch to my forehead and the words: "You ain't been through nothing; you ain't been through nothing." I know that this was only the devil trying to use my brother to do his dirty work. As a person who had gone through nothing, why was I still dealing with the effects of my son's recent recovery from kidney surgery, finding out my husband was secretly communicating with a possible daughter I never knew about, and losing a major business contract that was a significant portion of our income. Yet I still had to smile on the outside when I was completely engulfed with the pain of depression on the inside. It was like having to hold a mouth full of vomit with nowhere for it to spew out freely. I thought that I would never be able to move forward sharing the good times of life with my brother again. I cried for days, not knowing what I had done to cause it and how I should have been strong enough to walk away. I recognized that it was just the devil trying to tear us apart because he knew that my vulnerability was my family. The devil knew that my heart was changing and I was longing to come closer to Christ. But thank God that as days and weeks passed, even though we never talked about it again, we both knew that we could never live without loving each other. I am one that says texting is a coward's way out, but this time I appreciated that text from my brother. It was at that moment, after a couple exchanges of messages, we both understood that we had to accept that everyone doesn't think the same and that we have to respect each other and know that it is ok to agree to disagree. If the devil had had his way in this situation, trying to challenge the old me, the steak knife next to some old pancakes on the table could have changed this story completely. Thank God for covering us.

I was starting to write again when this happened, but I stopped for almost a year because, even though this and other issues were resolved, it took quite a while for the pain to not completely go away, but subside. But, as I said, sometimes we have to take a pause or completely remove ourselves from negative, destructive distractions that take you off the course of prosperity. Run for cover, and God will provide the perfect shield.

just forget about it

I am so glad that God gave me a forgetful mind for most of the bad things that have happened in my life. I can recall that something had happened, but after a while, could never recall any of the details. I have categorized this as another one of my God-given protection plans to save me from expressing myself in such a negative manner; it would cause hurt and pain to someone else and ultimately destruction for me. Believe me, for a while I was really considering writing a sequel to Steve Harvey's book and calling it, "Act Like a Woman, Drink Like a Man." Thank God for PMS, Productive Memory Selection.

goodbye negative

For every negative there is a positive. We have got to stop running towards what appears to be the easiest path, like not reading instructions before beginning a project. Not reading the Bible because you hate reading, but instead displaying it everywhere you go. You have to spiritually force-feed yourself with the Word if reading is one of your weaknesses. The laziest way is never the best and your success will be short-lived, if you are successful at all. We have got to learn to practice facing our weaknesses. We have the power to re-invent ourselves and fill our lives with positivity, and wipe out the laziness and negativity we have inexcusably come accustomed to holding on to.

momma needs me a necessary distraction but come right back karen, come right back.

If you are tired of the same old "same old," try new things in Jesus' name. Ask yourself, "What can I do productively today, that will create a positive future of prosperity tomorrow?"

do i know you?

Just as you have got to be able to recognize a **F.L.U.** carrier, don't allow yourself to be used as a negative instrument with carrier tendencies. Let me tell you this and maybe it will help you understand better. What you see in the mirror can be so different than what someone else sees. For example, you are out and about and someone compliments you and tells you that you look great. You are not able to receive the compliment sincerely because when you took that last look in the mirror before you left home, you did not see what they saw. You saw someone totally different than the one who was complimented. That is because you only allowed your eyes to focus on the "you" of self-pity and not the "you" of joy. True story: after being visited by a friend one day, she told me that I looked great. I didn't even say thank you because I was skeptical about what she was saying. The moment she left, standing in front of my biggest critic, the mirror, I looked deep into my eyes and saw all the way inside of me. I saw the stuff that make-up couldn't cover up. The memories of my past were viscously oppressing any hopes for my future. I was a dressed-up mess. I now had reached my breaking point. I broke down and cried profusely. I cried so hard and so long, just looking at myself in total silence. I kept crying and saying to God that it was so hard to believe because I just couldn't see Him; I just couldn't feel Him. At that moment, after doing all of that productive crying, I heard the wind from my breath and instantly understood that there is so much that we believe that we cannot see, so why was I making it so hard to believe in God Almighty? Suddenly, there was a voice that came to me that said, "Karen, get ready, change is getting ready to happen; you better get ready because change is getting ready to happen." Now, don't get ahead of me and think that I am about to say that I heard God speaking to me, because you would be wrong. As a matter of fact, knowing that I am still growing, if it was God's voice that I heard, I probably would not have heard all He had to say, because I most likely would have taken off running out of my house. But anyway, to me the voice, without question, was definitely recognizable. It was the voice God gave to me: my own. It was at that very moment I knew that Karen was ready for change. When I look at myself now, I always see a "great work in progress."

Use your mirror as a counseling tool that can keep the connection between you and God. Stop riding the waves of failure and complaints and get on the joy ride of prosperity. So from this day forward, if someone sees you talking to yourself and says that it's alright as long as you don't answer back, tell them that you have to because you are waiting on an answer. Think about it: If talking to yourself is so bad, why do all of us have the ability to do it, and most of us frequently engage in it? I truly believe it is necessary. So with that being said, it is a permanent part of me, and I love it. If you don't believe me, ask those that work around me. I am so glad that I finally recognized that the light was left on for me! But, as I keep trying to tell you, I am still growing.

IDEAS/NOTE TO SELF

Why Can't Some People Get Rid of the F.L.U.?

Chapter 8

WHY CAN'T SOME PEOPLE GET RID OF THE F.L.U.?

There are some people that just simply refuse to believe in God; some consciously and some unconsciously. They believe that they are truly in control of their lives. They believe that God does not exist because so many bad things are happening in the world that God should be able to control and stop. Many people will never accept the fact that their "choice" to make decisions is by His grace. Just as God allowed Adam and Eve to make the choice to eat of the tree of life after He warned them not to eat of it, He has given the same power of choice to believers and non-believers alike. Even though making the choice may be easy, dealing with the consequences of your choice is a totally different ball game. My youngest son was watching television one day and a minister was talking about the subject "for better or worse." He asked me if I said these words when his dad and I married. I told him yes. He looked at me and said, "Well, I choose better." Now, I am not sure if he really understood what he was saying, but the revelation it brought to me was amazing. One thing you need to always remember is that we all have to wear the face of a bad decision. Do you really want to understand why bad things so easily happen? Now see, you are thinking too hard when the answer is very simple: because it's not hard to make stupid decisions. No matter how many options you may have, you must choose "better."

do what for you?

Why is it, when someone says that something is free we jump right in not even knowing what it is, how it works, or how it tastes, but we can't do this when it comes to Salvation and God's promises that are always absolutely free? There are so many selfish, closed-minded people in the world that just cannot see what God has in store for them. Therefore, they will never be able to free themselves from the **F.L.U.** Because of their broken character, they will never do for someone else first. They never think that they are using anybody because they feel like everyone owes them something. They are only going to do just enough to get by. You cannot get them to give away anything and the only help they will offer is discouraging words when someone else is trying to move forward. Their primary goal is to block the way or hold you down and then blame God for your shortcoming. They would rather climb a tree and tell a lie to you than stand on the ground and tell the truth.

Lord the older i get the smarter my parents are; if I had only listened...

keep writing karen keep writing

[72]

One thing that I tend to say, which people that are spiritually close to me have heard: "Can you push me up, trusting I will turn around and pull you up?" Everyone may not be ready for movement at the same time, but the "crab in a bucket" mentality makes movement hard for so many that are truly ready to go after their dreams and receive their blessings. These crabs can disguise themselves as our parents, spouses, children, significant others, classmates of our children, teachers, friends, co-workers, church members, and so on. They camouflage themselves so carefully and are usually those that are closely connected to us.

Case in point; check this out. My daughter has been in the kitchen literally since she was two years old. Everyone that knows her understands the depth of her passion and her dream to one day become her own boss and grow into having a highly successful business. Cooking has always been her passion. Just recently, she made that big leap of faith to step out and start selling her products to family and friends and start saving to invest in a building for her business. She visited one of our local neighborhood businesses just knowing that the support would definitely be there. When she asked both of the workers if they wanted to buy a gourmet candy apple, one replied, "how much?" When she told him the price, he acted as if a $5.00 stick-up was about to take place. She asked him did he not think it was worth it, and he responded in a very cold manner, "not to me." Now considering she knew this person and had pretty close ties to him through family, she was really disappointed at his reaction and started to doubt herself and her work. Thank God the other worker thought differently and generously supported her. But there was still the question of "quality of work" in her mind when someone she knew responded so negatively about it. What if she did not have many others for moral support to push her forward at this point? After all, if someone she knew wouldn't buy, why would a stranger? Right now is where the crab could have very well succeeded and snuffed out her flame to pursue her dream of becoming her own boss. Now if anyone should have supported her, it should have been him who was once in her shoes; starting from the bottom.

We frequently ask the question, what is happening to our young people? Well I have one answer for you. It is because our older generation is not conscience of the message they are sending to our younger generation that hard work doesn't pay off and their dreams are not real enough to become reality. Before we speak our opinion to them, remember this saying I read years ago that goes something like this: a person is just like a board that has been pierced by a nail; even though you pull the nail out and cosmetically fill in the hole, the hole is still there. You may apologize later, but it does not cover the hole that you emotionally embedded into that person. Remember we all start from the bottom and can fall back down. The biggest problem will be what or whom you will have to face when you look up. Be a fire starter and not a fire extinguisher. And a note to the one feeling discouraged right now about a dream that seems to be slipping away: remember, when God calls you to do something that benefits you, your existing circumstances are of no regard to Him. He will make sure the right people are in the right places to have favor on you at just the right time. Miracles don't stop at birth. They can happen as often as the tick on a clock. We have got to stop worrying about the "why's" and the "what if's" and concentrate on the "what is."

three out of our four vehicles have broken down and my dad's borrowed truck break lights won't go off now after using it one day. keep writing karen keep writing

window shopper

Don't be that person that desires being in the presence of successful people and only go home and wishing it were you. Do something about it. Use those people as valuable resources or creative tools to get you where you want to be. Be able to follow, as long as they are taking you in the right direction. Take on the sight of an eagle and see keenly far in the distance what you have the potential to get, even though it seems to be far away. Keeping a bird's-eye view makes the getting feel so good. Surround yourself with people with a purpose. Remember, waiting for success to happen is like waiting for a check in the mail. Why wait when you know you haven't worked for it? Keep working your daytime job while you search for and conquer your dream. Remember, a job does not define who you are; it only represents what you do. If you can't do it this way, throw in the towel and step out on Faith. I did it once eight years ago, and it changed my life - until I lost my way - but that was not God's fault. I am wearing that mask of a bad decision right now, but I am in fast forward mode of "still growing, cleaning myself up, and doing it again." We all are spiritually equipped with the insight to fight all useless, meaningless distractions. Use it! And remember this little saying that I say to myself all the time: "If a man doesn't work he doesn't eat; so how hungry are you?" Prosperity is just sitting there waiting for a ride. Don't let someone else beat you to your paying passenger.

The Bible tells us that the poor will be with us always, so please understand that some of the poor have made the "choice" to be poor by preferring to be a possessor of the **F.L.U.** and not using the tools that God equipped them with to be some of the most successful people in the world. God is in every one of us; some just refuse to believe it. There have been so many times when I have gotten some of the best ideas and heard some of the most amazing things from some of the worst people. Some will continue being a hoarder of gifts and talents. They will never share them with family, friends, neighbors, or the world for that matter, to see how powerful they really are. If we could take a key and open the spiritual door inside of us, it would be jaw-dropping to see how many talents and gifts we have stored away inside each of us. Stop going shopping for prosperity

[76]

and only looking through the window. Go ahead and get what you want. Don't settle for being a window shopper.

How Do I Keep Myself Healthy After the F.L.U.?

Chapter 9

HOW DO I KEEP MYSELF HEALTHY AFTER THE F.L.U.?

I Corinthians 6:19 tells us that your body is a temple of the Holy Spirit which lives in you, and was given to you by God. You do not belong to yourself. We must honor and glorify God with our bodies. If you suffer from depression, just as we think ourselves into depression, we have got to start thinking ourselves into prosperity, happiness, increase, and favor. I call it "thought replacement therapy." Every time you think about something negative, replace that thought with something positive that you can enjoy at that moment or in the future. Limit your exposure to negativity and remove yourself from watching television shows consumed with violence. Don't keep the channel tuned in to the news all the time. These things play a large role in the negativity and depression that we feel inside, and it incapacitates your productive and creative abilities, which ultimately decapitates you, suffocating all of your gifts and talents. Some people experience depression in a greater capacity than others. Don't deny yourself professional help if you feel you need it. Remember that God has given helping and healing powers through the hands of man. So get some help and keep it moving. Tell anyone with negative intent that your misery no longer requires company and that you will no longer be partly cloudy, but sunny all day. Understanding and knowing your imperfections and accepting them are what make you perfect. If anyone dwells on what they consider your imperfections, you just simply tell them that even with your imperfections, you know what you are not: a failure. The only reason they dwell on your imperfections is because deep down inside they are comparing themselves to you which means, they have put you above them. Amazing!

motivate yourself

Being mindful of your company is an absolute must. If you are unsure and really want to know a person's true character, catch them when they think nobody is listening or looking. Even if they are not speaking, their body language and most definitely their eyes will display their character. Remember to stay motivated. Motivation is like exercise, and you tend to do better when there is someone with you because you don't want that person to see you quit. Find someone that you have faith-based interests with and build upon each other and keep each other encouraged and inspired. WHERE THERE IS A WILL, THERE IS A WINNER!

One day when I asked my son about school, he told me he made an "A" on his homework assignment. I asked a question without thinking: "Did you do all of the work?" In a very respectful yet sarcastic tone he replied, "One thing about homework, you can't do half and get an 'A' as a grade." Wise words indeed from a child, and we should use this same concept and apply it to our lives. Do your best and do it all! Don't let anyone talk you down. Don't look

[80]

for a pat on the back for trying when you did not complete what you set out to finish. Try again and keep pushing forward. When fear kicks in, just remember this: If there were no obstacles, there would be no high jumpers. Don't let fear stop you from moving forward. Always remember, everyone is afraid of heights when they are falling and afraid of water when they are drowning. Fear is normal, but conquerable.

watching anniversary of march on

washington president Barack Obama

speaking necessary distraction.

keep writing, karen keep writing

me time

As married women, we need to reach out to other women, whether they are single or married, children or not, and start meeting at least once a month to speak about things that we want to do in life but have not been able to take that first step for fear of falling (failing). Wives, announce to your family that you are also a part of your family and take your "me time" back. Because we are nurturers by nature, we can become so entrapped with protecting everyone else that we lose our own identity. Take it back and go after your dreams. Don't allow the demands of your family to cripple you. You will find yourself to be a better mother than before. Your dedication to your dream and seeing the positive results of it will cause everyone else in the household to pursue their dreams because of the happiness and excitement they now see in you. It will become contagious! Make the strength of your family work for you.

let me out of here!

Do not allow anger to be a part of your character. It is like being locked in a smoke-filled room with no windows or doors. It totally consumes you until you die! I can remember when I had a temper from hell, and the devil would just be sitting on the edge of my tongue with a bowl of popcorn waiting on the main event. Even though through the years I outgrew this negative personality, I found out that it could still be in you, and being around other negative factors could stir it right back up if you allow yourself too much exposure to it. Years ago, when I worked for 911 emergency and was around others who used a lot of foul language, I started cursing like a sailor, and could put together words that would even make the devil himself ashamed. Once I found another job and separated myself from that environment, I then became conscience of my words and did not want to go back to that way of talking. You just have to stay away and avoid things that cause negativity in your life, because you can very easily fall back into a destructive way of living. As we interact daily, whether it is at work, church, leisure, etc., we are like magnetic objects attracting other people to us. However, it is still up to you whether you will attract negative or positive people. This idea is related to the saying that birds of a feather flock together. It is up to you to be a positive attraction and not a negative one.

When captivated by something, you must think first and use that sixth sense that God gave you: common sense. If you are unsure about the way something looks, look again. If you are not sure about the way something feels, think again about how you feel. If you think you are in the wrong place, RUN!

It's going to work out. thank you Lord for opening our eyes, a necessary distraction...

keep writing karen keep writing

healing brings prosperity

Believing (which is the first step in healing) that God has given you great potential for success is the golden key to opportunity and financial increase. Even though you have to operate in the world, do not let the world consume you. Be who you are, and that is a child of the King Himself. Don't let anyone tell you not to believe in Him just because they have their own doubts and questions. Believing that character really does speak volumes about a person's inner being; remember Psalms 37:4-5: by delighting yourself in the Lord and believing that He will be delighted in you... There is never "no way out" when there is God. You may lose some things as you are going through life, but as we travel with Him, He disposes of all the junk along the way. He removes all the trash so that you will be able to walk lighter, and not be weighed down with the past after he brings you through. Always remember that mistakes happen, but we learn from them.

Yes, just as Psalms 34:19 tells us, the good man does not escape all troubles because he has them, too. But the Lord helps all of us, and He even protects us from accidents. Leaning on His promises reminds me of laying my head on my grandmother's lap: protected and completely safe. I would like to share something with you before I move on. Earlier this year, I had a dream about my grandmother. In the dream I was walking down the street with a friend, one block over from my parent's home. I saw a lady standing in the window of her kitchen. Chills came all over me as I told my friend that the lady in the window was my grandmother. He and I both knew that my grandmother had died when I was about eleven years old. I insisted on knocking on the door so I did. She opened the door. Now, in the dream I was 100% sure that this was my grandmother, even though I could never see a face. She proceeded to sit down in a chair at the edge of the walkway in her yard. As I hugged her, there was such a strong feeling of peace and comfort that completely overwhelmed me and I just couldn't turn her loose; I felt that if I let her go, this feeling would leave me forever and it was a feeling that one would want to possess forever; a feeling of total peace. If I let her go, I would be letting this feeling go forever for I knew she was really no longer here. As I was holding on so tightly to her she whispered in my ear, "I am not your grandmother." Feeling her body in my arms, I could tell that she was a stout woman; whom my grandmother was not, but I couldn't let her go. Even though I heard her voice which was not my grandmothers, I couldn't let her go. I was crying profusely with joy. I can only describe the peace and protection that I felt as a moment in heaven, and I did not ever want to let her go. Suddenly I woke up and my nose was bleeding uncontrollably. I called my sister and was crying as I told her about the dream. The words that I was telling her just weren't strong enough for her to visualize the dream as I felt it, but she listened and understood. Periodically from that day to this one, I will cry when I think of how I truly felt when she held me in the dream. I would have stayed there forever but I was unconsciously awakened. My Aunt Honey passed away two days after this dream. She was a stout woman, daughter of my grandmother, and a confessed child of God. Even though she was blind, two days before her death, the day of my dream, she was able to see everything in her hospital room. God has a way of speaking and revealing things to us. His Love is as beautiful and intimate as the sunlight hugging the edge of a cloud. Don't try to put reasoning behind every decision you make when it comes to your relationship with Christ.

Some things are not understandable at that particular moment, but acceptably good for us. Remember, God does not work in mysterious ways. He works in unexplainable, miraculous ways. Our minds are just too small to understand how many ways He can handle one small or large situation.

Prosperity is yours right now. Believe that without further explanation, before you lose out by trying to understand the same thing in different ways. I was once, twice, three…well, too many times to count, in situations that I would give to God to handle and then would turn around, when the clock was too close to the cutoff time, and try to fix it myself. I felt He could do it, but His timing was just a little off, so I would try to fix it myself. MISTAKE! If only I had gone to sleep, stayed asleep, and let Him work, I would have been able to tell you how good the situation worked out. But I can't. I didn't let Him help me. And all of these mistakes you have read so far are a reflection of just that. Not letting my Father protect me when He promised me He would. Crazy, isn't it? Just crazy! Now, this is coming from someone who, until now, had not yet put her life in line with God's plan, but is working on it. I need to pick up the speed. So with this being said, I have a true message of inspirational knowledge for you. IF YOU DON'T LET HIM WORK, HE WON'T. We have tried the wrong way long enough. It's time to step out and do it right, expecting right to happen for us. As I said before, we have to stop believing that bad things can happen all the time and doubting that great things can expectantly happen in our lives each and every day.

[86]

hmmmmmm?????

Think about this: God made our hands and feet to have the same structure for balance and protection. He created the same look inside the palm of our hands as on the soles of our feet, which is totally different from all the other skin on our body. Awesome! Feet made tough enough to stand boldly, and hands strong enough to hold firmly. If God was great enough to create us with such intimate details, He is great enough for you to ask Him anything and expect Him to hold true to His promises to you. You will no longer find a need to ask everyone else who was also created by God, questions about yourself.

if you feel like your dreams are on your shoulders feeling lost and all alone, take them down; welcome them home and give them a great big hug!

keep writing karen, keep writing

You have a direct communication line assigned specifically to you. You no longer have to sit around holding your head in your hands. There is always a way out of any situation. Your life can be as beautiful as an early morning sunrise. Start every day with a "good morning talk" to your Maker and a "hello welcoming" to prosperity. YOU ARE ON YOUR WAY!

God did not give me these words, designs, and captions for this book to draw attention to me. The idea is not to say

[87]

"Wow! I did not know she had it in her!" Instead the prosperity will come from you saying, "Wow! I did not know I have it in me!"

Here is one last thought for you to ponder. Have you ever had an idea come to you from what seems like nowhere, and you are overwhelmed with excitement and passion about it? That is God blessing you with a purpose for your gift, and high-fiving you for receiving it. When the fire stops burning because you have procrastinated too long, God has probably moved that gift to someone else instead of letting it sit and die. The answer to finding success is not looking for another job with better pay, but it is pursuing that inner force that is calling you to take a closer look at it and follow its direction. Remember, if it is God-given it has to be born, whether through you or someone else. Don't allow the negative distractions to stop you any longer.

phone messaged: karen i got a complaint that is probably a few weeks old that the ladies bathroom was not cleaned well. one complaint; weeks old; and bathroom used all of fourteen hours before we get there; really! stop writing karen and put a period on it. it's time to shine and leave the past behind.

IDEAS/NOTE TO SELF

Filling In the Blanks

Chapter 10

FILLING IN THE BLANKS

Stop for a few minutes before putting this book to the side and meditate. Get into your deepest thoughts and write about one thing that can help start filling in the blanks of your life. Don't try to fool yourself. We all have them and we all can use some help. **IF YOU WRITE IT, YOU CAN FIX IT. NOT WRITING IT MEANS YOU ARE WILLING TO STAY IN DENIAL OF THE BLANKS IN YOUR LIFE. LET'S DO IT; YOU HAVE A WHOLE PAGE TO YOURSELF. I WILL EVEN HELP YOU GET STARTED:**

Looking at my life Lord, help me ……………

Give me ………….

Lead me ………………

Make me …………………..

Your gifts and talents are designed especially for you.
Don't abuse them. Use them

[91]

TOP 25 ANSWERS

Through Texting and social media, I asked this question to see what type of responses I would get:

What is the number one reason you have not followed your dream that can or would have lead you to a financially successful future for you that you could see yourself enjoying with your family and ultimately leaving to your children and grandchildren?

1. I don't think I have the ability to do something well enough to succeed on my own
2. Finance
3. Lazy
4. Not able to jump out on Faith
5. Guaranteed backup plan
6. What if
7. Comfort zone
8. Became a man too early; family first
9. Never actually thought about being extremely rich
10. Hoping I don't have to leave my children anything
11. Fear of end result not materializing as planned
12. Fear of letting go of what you presently have
13. Not able to communicate well enough
14. I have too much going on
15. Not enough capital
16. My history has messed it up for me
17. Not enough time in a day when you have a family

18. My credit is butchered
19. I don't know enough people to make it work
20. Not being able to do it because of taking care of family members
21. Need more money
22. I do not have enough experience
23. I never want to jeopardize neglecting my family when trying to fulfill a personal dream
24. Too much going on right now
25. When I was younger it was fear, not that I am older it is money and time

Understanding that failure should not be an option, do not give up on a dream by creating artificial barriers. There is work and sacrifice involved but YOU CAN DO IT! I purposely placed the pictures with the "distractions" comments for you to see that even though my life was filled with a lot of problems, I never stopped writing. DON'T GIVE UP! Figure out what it is you dream of doing, what is in the way, and how to get rid of it. Speaking from experience, I really understand when you think to yourself, "It's not as easy as it sound." However, I refuse to give up. Find a starting point. One suggestion I have is to start using some of our social media time to focus more on ourselves than others. Challenge yourself to cut this time in half and most of you will have rewarded yourself with at least one hour per day. Don't go through life trying to make yourself and others believe that the life you have is the life you wanted.

THIS IS MY CHALLENGE TO YOU

YOU ARE A CHILD OF THE KING!

SLAVES WERE MADE TO LOOK DOWN.

ARE YOU LOOKING UP?

Enjoy us on the web at:

www.makinglifelarge.com

PERSONAL CHALLENGE

www.ingramcontent.com/pod-product-compliance
Lightning Source LLC
Chambersburg PA
CBHW071013040426
42443CB00007B/758